Contents

1 Chapter 1: Fractured Beginnings

The world felt unsafe, a constant tremor beneath my feet. It wasn't a single event, but a slow, insidious erosion of trust, a chilling wind that whispered doubts into my young mind. The mundane became terrifying; the ordinary, a threat. A misplaced toy, a harsh word, a sudden silence – each held the potential for a cascade of fear, a tightening in my chest that made breathing difficult. The foundation of my sense of self, still so fragile, began to crumble under the weight of these early experiences. I learned to shrink, to become invisible, to anticipate the next blow. Survival became a silent, solitary endeavor. My own internal landscape mirrored the fractured world around me, a jigsaw puzzle with vital pieces missing.

Childhood should be a sanctuary, a time of carefree exploration and joyful discovery. Instead, my memories are fragmented, stitched together with threads of apprehension and unease. The vibrant colors of innocence were dulled, replaced by the muted tones of apprehension. Games became fraught with anxiety, friendships fragile and conditional, laughter tainted with a lingering sense of dread. The world of make-believe offered a temporary escape, but even there, shadows lurked, mirroring the unspoken anxieties that permeated my reality. The loss wasn't just of a carefree childhood; it was the loss of an untainted belief in the inherent goodness of the world, a loss that left an aching void in its wake.

The impact of these early experiences wasn't just about immediate emotional pain; they laid the groundwork for a lifetime of struggles. My capacity for trust was damaged, replaced by a deep-seated wariness that colored every relationship. Simple interactions became minefields, each requiring careful navigation, a constant vigilance against potential harm. Intimacy felt dangerous, vulnerability a weakness to be avoided at all costs. I built walls, high and impenetrable, protecting myself from the pain of further betrayal. Yet, these defenses, meant to safeguard my heart, imprisoned me as well, isolating me from the warmth and connection I so desperately craved. My emotional responses often felt disproportionate, extreme, a testament to the fragility of my inner world.

Healing doesn't begin with the absence of pain; it begins with the acknowledgement of it, a painful but necessary step towards liberation. It's in confronting these early wounds, in naming them and understanding their impact, that we begin to reclaim our narrative. This is not about assigning blame or dwelling on the past; it's about understanding how those experiences have shaped us, how they continue to influence our perceptions and behaviors. The path to healing is rarely linear; it's a winding road with setbacks and breakthroughs, moments of clarity interwoven with periods of profound doubt. This initial recognition is the crucial first step, a kindling of hope in the midst of darkness. It acknowledges the suffering without being overwhelmed by it, leaving space for the possibility of growth and transformation.

We must remember that healing is a personal journey; there is no one-size-fits-all solution. What works for one person may not work for another. It's crucial to find what resonates with you—whether that's therapy, meditation, journaling, spending time in nature, or connecting with supportive friends and family. The essential ingredient is self-compassion, a recognition that our struggles are valid and that we deserve kindness and understanding, particularly during difficult times. It requires patience, self-awareness, and a willingness to confront our deepest fears and vulnerabilities, a commitment to peeling back the layers of defense that have protected—and yet also imprisoned—us. Self-compassion is not self-indulgence; rather, it is the foundation of genuine change and the key to unlocking our innate capacity for growth.

This chapter is not merely an exploration of past traumas; it's a crucial foundation for understanding the journey ahead. The fractured beginnings discussed here are not an insurmountable barrier but rather a starting point, a springboard from which we can begin to build a more resilient and fulfilling life. By understanding the roots of our suffering, we gain the power to shape a healthier and more compassionate future for ourselves. Recognizing the past allows us to embrace the present with a renewed sense of hope, moving forward not as victims, but as survivors, stronger and wiser, having navigated the treacherous path to healing and self-discovery. This journey begins with acceptance, with the understanding that we are not alone and that healing is indeed possible.

1.1 Early Trauma

Early experiences profoundly shape us, leaving indelible marks on our emotional landscapes. For some, these marks are subtle, barely perceptible ripples in the otherwise calm waters of life. For others, however, these early experiences manifest as a catastrophic tsunami, leaving behind a wreckage of shattered self-esteem, crippling anxiety, and persistent feelings of inadequacy. The impact of early trauma, whether it stems from neglect, abuse, or witnessing violence, can significantly impede personal growth and happiness throughout life. Understanding these effects is crucial for beginning the healing journey.

The consequences of early trauma are multifaceted and far-reaching. It's not simply a matter of "getting over it." Instead, the effects can subtly or overtly impact various aspects of an individual's life, often manifesting in unexpected ways. Relationships may be strained by a deep-seated mistrust or fear of intimacy. Professional success may be hindered by anxiety or difficulties in managing stress effectively. Physical ailments can even emerge as a result of prolonged stress and emotional turmoil. These effects often go unnoticed or misattributed, delaying the crucial step of seeking help.

Children are particularly vulnerable. Their brains are still developing, and they lack the cognitive tools and life experiences necessary to fully process and cope with traumatic events. What an adult might rationalize or contextualize, a child might internalize as a fundamental flaw in themselves or the world around them. This internalization can lead to a distorted perception of self and reality, fostering negative self-image and contributing to future mental health challenges. The absence of a secure and loving environment during these formative years exacerbates the trauma's effects.

Recognizing the signs of early trauma is the first crucial step toward healing. These signs may not always be obvious. Some individuals might present with outwardly successful lives, masking deep-seated emotional pain and dysfunction. Others might struggle with substance abuse, self-harm, or persistent anxiety and depression. A lack of trust, difficulty forming healthy relationships, or a consistent sense of being "on edge" are also common indicators. Professional guidance is invaluable in identifying these subtle yet significant signs.

Seeking help is not a sign of weakness; it's a testament to strength and a commitment to well-being. Ignoring the effects of early trauma only allows it to fester and potentially worsen over time. Therapy offers a safe and supportive environment to unpack these painful experiences, process them in a healthy way, and develop coping mechanisms. Different therapeutic approaches, such as trauma-focused cognitive behavioral therapy (TF-CBT) or eye movement desensitization and reprocessing (EMDR), are specifically designed to address the unique challenges presented by trauma. Choosing the right therapist is vital, and it often involves trial and error until finding the right fit.

Beyond professional therapy, fostering self-compassion is crucial. Treating yourself with the same kindness and understanding you would offer a close friend is essential. This doesn't mean ignoring the pain or minimizing the trauma; rather, it involves acknowledging the impact it has had and validating your feelings without self-criticism or judgment. Engage in self-care practices that nourish your mind, body, and spirit. This could encompass anything from regular exercise and a balanced diet to mindfulness meditation and engaging in hobbies that bring joy.

Remember that healing is a journey, not a destination. It's a process that requires patience, perseverance, and self-compassion. There will be setbacks, and that's okay. The key is to learn from these experiences, adjust your approach if needed, and continue moving forward. Don't be afraid to seek additional support from loved ones, support groups, or spiritual advisors. Building a strong support network can make a significant difference in your journey to healing. Your resilience and strength are greater than you might realize. The path to healing from early trauma is long, but the destination, a life filled with serenity and peace, is well worth the effort. Your future is not defined by your past; you have the power to shape a healthier and happier life for yourself. The healing process is a testament to your courage and your innate capacity for growth and recovery. Your journey is uniquely yours, and remember that seeking help is a powerful act of self-love and a vital step towards reclaiming your life.

1.2 Lost Innocence

The stolen innocence of childhood, a violation so profound it leaves an indelible mark on the soul, isn't simply a fading memory; it's a silent architect of the self. This isn't about assigning blame, but acknowledging the brutal reality: that the carefree days of youth were shattered, leaving behind a landscape of fear, confusion, and a deep sense of betrayal. The impact reverberates through life, influencing relationships, choices, and even the way we perceive the world around us. This is the foundational crack in the edifice of our being.

Understanding this loss isn't about wallowing in the past. It's about recognizing its power, its insidious ability to shape our present. It's about seeing how that shattered trust continues to manifest—in our hesitancy to form bonds, our hypervigilance, the subtle ways in which we anticipate pain. For many, it's the unseen hand pulling the strings of their daily lives, influencing reactions that may seem inexplicable to those who haven't experienced such profound violation. This chapter is your first step in understanding that unseen hand.

Trauma isn't always a dramatic event; sometimes it's the slow drip of neglect, the consistent undermining of self-worth, the absence of safety and unconditional love. These experiences, subtle yet pervasive, can erode the very foundation of a child's sense of self, leaving a void that shapes their adult life. Imagine a child who experiences constant criticism, their efforts consistently dismissed, their innate curiosity stifled. The result isn't simply a bruised ego; it's a fundamental sense of inadequacy that can persist long into adulthood, coloring perceptions and limiting possibilities. It's a heavy burden to bear.

The impact on adult relationships is significant. The initial loss of trust, of secure attachment, makes forming healthy relationships challenging. Those who experienced early trauma may find themselves constantly seeking validation, plagued by insecurities, or struggling with intimacy. The fear of betrayal can loom large, creating distance where connection should thrive. They may struggle to identify true love and affection, often confusing codependency with genuine connection. They might fear letting their guard down, constantly looking for any threat.

Furthermore, the struggle with self-worth is often a pervasive symptom of lost innocence. The belief in one's inherent goodness, the feeling of being loved and valued unconditionally—these cornerstones of a healthy self-image—can be irrevocably damaged. The ensuing feelings of inadequacy, of being fundamentally flawed, can be devastating. This isn't a conscious decision; it's a deep-seated wound impacting subconscious beliefs that profoundly influence behavior. It's a silent battle within the self that often goes unrecognized until consciously addressed.

Recognizing these patterns is crucial to embarking on the healing journey. It's not about dwelling on the pain, but about understanding its impact, identifying its manifestations, and learning to manage its influence. This acknowledgment, this conscious recognition of the trauma's footprint on your life, is the essential first step. Only by understanding this pervasive effect can one begin the work of healing and rebuilding a stronger, more resilient self. This journey is not linear; it's a long winding road filled with unexpected detours and hard-fought victories. But the path forward starts with honest self-reflection.

The road to healing will be challenging, that much is certain. However, it's a journey not to be undertaken in isolation. Seek support from therapists, support groups, or trusted friends and family. Allow yourself to be vulnerable; let others in. The power of human connection, the sharing of experiences, the realization that you are not alone in your struggle, can be profoundly healing. Remember that healing isn't about erasing the past; it's about integrating it, learning from it, and finding ways to move forward with grace and resilience. Your story isn't over; it's just beginning.

2 Chapter 2: The Weight of Scars

Lingering pain isn't always visible; a deep cut might heal, leaving a barely-there scar, while an unseen emotional wound festers. This isn't about physical injuries alone, though they carry their own weight. Consider the child who falls, scraping their knee; the physical sting fades, but the memory of fear, of vulnerability, might remain, shaping their future reactions to falls, to perceived threats, even to intimacy. The weight of such experiences, often subtly woven into the fabric of our being, can become a pervasive influence.

Emotional scars are far more insidious. They're the lingering effects of betrayal, the echoes of harsh words spoken in anger, the chilling memories of neglect or abuse. They manifest in various ways: a constant feeling of unease, a crippling inability to trust, or a pervasive sense of self-doubt. These aren't just fleeting feelings; they're deeply ingrained patterns of thinking and behaving, subtly influencing decisions, relationships, and overall well-being. They can lead to avoidance, isolation, and even depression, silently undermining our lives. They can colour how we perceive ourselves and our place in the world, shaping our expectations and hindering our potential.

Mental barriers often accompany these emotional wounds, acting as shields against further hurt. They might manifest as anxiety, fear of intimacy, or an inability to form healthy attachments. These aren't deliberate choices; they are defensive mechanisms the mind develops to protect itself from further pain. Imagine a fortress built around a vulnerable heart, its walls thick and high, protecting against potential threats but also barring access to joy, connection, and genuine intimacy. Breaking down these walls is vital, but it is a journey requiring immense courage and self-compassion. This isn't a simple task; it often takes years of dedicated work, and it's rarely a linear process. Many people struggle with this, and there is no shame in seeking help from professionals.

Understanding these scars—their origins, their manifestations, and their impact—is the first step toward healing. It's about acknowledging the past without being consumed by it. It's about recognizing that the weight of these experiences doesn't define who you are, but it certainly has shaped who you've become. This acknowledgement is crucial; it's the foundation upon which you build your path towards serenity. The road ahead might be long and arduous, filled with moments of doubt and setbacks, but the journey is undeniably worth undertaking. It's a journey of self-discovery, of reclaiming your life, and of learning to live with peace, even amidst the scars.

Many people struggle to understand the long-term consequences of past traumas. The initial trauma may seem distant, but its ripple effect continues to shape daily life. It's important to remember that healing is not about erasing the past; it's about integrating those experiences into a broader narrative, a narrative that acknowledges both pain and resilience. Recognizing that these scars are a part of your story allows you to view them with a degree of acceptance, lessening their power over your present and future. This understanding becomes your greatest ally, offering a new perspective from which to move forward. Take your time, it is okay to acknowledge you're still in pain and need help, reaching for support is not admitting defeat, instead, a step towards reclaiming your life.

The process of healing isn't always straightforward. It involves confronting painful memories, challenging ingrained thought patterns, and rebuilding trust in yourself and others. This isn't about forgetting; it's about finding ways to coexist with the past while creating a more peaceful present and future. This doesn't happen overnight; it takes time, patience, and a commitment to self-compassion. There will be days when you feel overwhelmed, days when the weight of your scars feels unbearable. Recognize these moments; don't judge yourself for them. Instead, acknowledge that these feelings are valid and deserve to be felt without judgment. Acceptance of this is a significant step in itself. It paves the way for healing and a more harmonious inner landscape.

Seeking professional help is not a sign of weakness; it is a sign of strength and self-awareness. Therapists and counselors can provide a safe and supportive space to explore these complex emotions, offering guidance and tools to navigate the challenges of living with trauma. They can help you to understand the root causes of your struggles, develop healthy coping mechanisms, and learn to manage overwhelming feelings. Remember that you do not have to go through this alone; many people have faced similar struggles and have found the strength and resilience to build fulfilling lives. You can also learn from the experiences of others and be guided by their pathways toward healing. Remember, that healing is not a linear process. There will be ups and downs. Be patient with yourself and celebrate your progress, no matter how small.

Remember that true healing requires a multifaceted approach that attends to all aspects of your well-being. Therefore, combining therapy with self-care practices, such as mindfulness, meditation, exercise, and healthy eating, can accelerate your healing journey. While each modality offers unique advantages, their combined application amplifies their effectiveness. Mindfulness, for instance, teaches you to be present in the moment, reducing the power of intrusive thoughts and memories. Regular exercise releases endorphins, naturally improving your mood and reducing stress levels. These are just two examples of supportive actions you can integrate into your daily routine to complement your healing journey. There are countless other ways to nourish your mind and body that will support your overall sense of well-being. The key is to find what resonates with you and to commit to a regular practice.

2.1 Lingering Pain

Lingering pain. It's a phantom limb, a constant thrum beneath the surface of daily life, a reminder of a past you may wish to forget but can't. It's not just physical; the emotional ache, the dull throbbing of unresolved trauma, can be far more debilitating. This pain, this weight, can manifest in countless ways – anxiety that clings like a shadow, outbursts of anger you don't understand, or a pervasive sense of emptiness that leaves you feeling profoundly alone, even amidst a crowd. You might find yourself constantly on edge, hyper-vigilant, flinching at unexpected noises or touches. Your sleep might be plagued by nightmares, and even during the day, vivid flashbacks might intrude, bringing the terror of the past back into the harsh light of the present.

These aren't simple bruises that heal with time. They are deep wounds, often invisible to the casual observer, yet causing profound and lasting damage. They impact every aspect of your being: relationships fracture under the strain, work performance suffers, and simple joys seem to lose their luster. You might isolate yourself, believing that no one could possibly understand your pain, or that you don't deserve connection or happiness. This isolation only serves to deepen the wounds, trapping you in a cycle of suffering that feels impossible to break.

Consider this: The mind and body are intricately connected. Physical pain can trigger emotional distress, and unresolved emotional trauma can manifest as physical symptoms. Chronic headaches, digestive problems, muscle tension, and sleep disturbances are all potential indicators of underlying emotional pain.

Ignoring these physical manifestations only allows the underlying emotional issues to fester and worsen. It's a vicious cycle, demanding attention and a holistic approach to healing.

So, where do you begin to address this lingering pain? It's not about magically erasing the past, but about learning to live with it, to integrate it into your narrative in a way that empowers you rather than defining you. Acknowledging the pain is the crucial first step. Don't minimize your experience; allow yourself to feel the full weight of what you've endured. This doesn't mean wallowing in self-pity, but rather giving yourself permission to grieve, to process, to confront the reality of your experiences.

Remember, you are not alone. Many people carry similar burdens, and there are countless resources available to help you navigate this difficult terrain. Professional help, whether through therapy or counseling, can provide a safe and supportive environment to explore your trauma, develop coping mechanisms, and learn healthier ways of relating to yourself and the world around you. Therapy isn't a sign of weakness; it's a courageous act of self-care, a recognition that you deserve support and healing. Therapists offer a range of approaches, from cognitive behavioral therapy (CBT) to trauma-focused therapies like EMDR (Eye Movement Desensitization and Reprocessing), and finding the right fit is essential for your progress. Don't be afraid to try different approaches until you find one that resonates with you. In addition to professional help, explore practices like mindfulness and meditation. These techniques can help you become more aware of your thoughts and feelings, allowing you to observe them without judgment. By developing a greater sense of self-awareness, you can begin to regulate your emotional responses and break free from the cycle of reactivity. Even short daily practices can make a significant difference. Start small – just five minutes a day – and gradually increase the duration as you become more comfortable.

Beyond professional help and mindfulness practices, consider connecting with others who understand what you're going through. Support groups provide a sense of community and shared experience, offering validation and a space to express yourself without judgment. Even talking to a trusted friend or family member can be immensely helpful. Remember, opening up about your pain doesn't make you weak; it makes you brave. It's a testament to your strength and your willingness to seek healing.

Finally, and perhaps most importantly, be patient and compassionate with yourself. Healing is a journey, not a destination. There will be good days and bad days, moments of progress and setbacks. Don't beat yourself up over the setbacks; rather, view them as opportunities to learn and grow. Celebrate the small victories, acknowledge your resilience, and remember that you are capable of overcoming this pain and building a life filled with peace, joy, and serenity. You deserve a life where the lingering pain fades into the background, replaced by a sense of wholeness and self-acceptance. This healing journey is yours alone, but you don't have to walk it alone. Remember that support is available, and that your path toward serenity is within reach.

2.2 Emotional Scars

Emotional pain, unlike a physical wound, often leaves no visible mark. Yet, its impact can be profound and enduring, shaping our perceptions, relationships, and overall well-being. These emotional scars, etched deep within our psyche, are the lingering echoes of past traumas, losses, and disappointments. They can manifest in countless ways, from crippling anxiety and debilitating depression to persistent feelings of anger, shame, or isolation. Understanding the nature and impact of these emotional scars is the first crucial step towards healing.

Many people carry the weight of unspoken traumas, events buried deep within their memories, influencing their present lives subtly or overtly. A seemingly minor trigger – a sound, a smell, even a fleeting memory – can send them spiraling back to the source of their pain. These triggers can be jarring and unpredictable, making daily life a minefield of potential emotional distress. Learning to recognize and manage these triggers is vital in navigating the path to recovery. It's a process of understanding the intricate connections between past experiences and present-day struggles.

The process of healing is deeply personal and rarely linear. It's not a simple matter of forgetting or erasing the past. Instead, it's about integrating the experiences into your life narrative, understanding how they shaped you, and finding ways to move forward without letting them define who you are. This means acknowledging the pain, validating your feelings, and gradually building a stronger, more resilient sense of self. It requires courage, self-compassion, and a willingness to confront difficult emotions.

Consider the metaphor of a garden ravaged by a storm. The destruction is immediate and obvious, but the aftermath demands consistent effort. You need to clear away the debris, tend to the injured plants, and nurture new growth. Similarly, healing from emotional scars is a gradual process that involves actively tending to your emotional well-being. This might involve seeking professional help, exploring different therapeutic approaches, or engaging in self-care practices that foster healing and growth.

Professional guidance can be invaluable in navigating the complexities of emotional scars. Therapists offer a safe and supportive space to process painful memories and develop healthy coping mechanisms. Different therapeutic modalities, such as cognitive behavioral therapy (CBT) or trauma-focused therapy, provide tailored approaches for addressing specific challenges. The right therapist can help you to identify the root causes of your emotional pain, challenge negative thought patterns, and learn to manage distressing emotions more effectively. This support system can significantly accelerate your journey to recovery.

Alongside professional help, mindfulness practices can prove remarkably effective in managing emotional distress. These techniques, rooted in ancient traditions, emphasize present-moment awareness, enabling you to observe your thoughts and feelings without judgment. Mindfulness exercises, such as meditation and deep breathing, can help to calm your nervous system, reduce anxiety, and increase emotional regulation. This heightened awareness can bring significant relief, and in turn empower you to better manage and regulate overwhelming emotions.

Remember, your journey to healing is unique to you. It will involve setbacks, moments of doubt, and perhaps even a reevaluation of your initial approaches. Don't be discouraged if you don't see immediate results. Healing from emotional scars takes time, patience, and self-compassion. Be kind to yourself throughout the process, celebrating small victories and acknowledging the progress you've made. Your healing is a testament to your strength and resilience. There is hope for a brighter future, a future where you are empowered to lead a more fulfilling life. Remember to focus on your progress not the perfection.

It's crucial to remember that you're not alone in this. Many people share similar experiences, and there's a vast network of support available to you. Don't hesitate to reach out to friends, family, or support groups. Connecting with others who understand can provide invaluable comfort, validation, and a sense of community. Sharing your experiences can be a powerful way to reduce feelings of isolation and shame, and begin the process of healing. Your journey to healing is about moving forward and developing a stronger sense of self.

The ultimate goal is not to erase the past but to integrate it into your life narrative in a way that empowers you to move forward. By embracing self-compassion, developing coping mechanisms, and nurturing your emotional well-being, you can transform your emotional scars into sources of strength and resilience. You can learn to live with serenity, contentment, and a profound sense of self-acceptance, even while acknowledging the profound impact of your past experiences. It is a long journey, but one that leads to a stronger, more compassionate, and ultimately more fulfilled you. Your story, and your journey to healing, is a testament to the strength of the human spirit, capable of transforming suffering into growth. Remember to celebrate every milestone along the way.

2.3 Mental Barriers

Negative thought patterns, often rooted in past experiences, can erect formidable mental barriers. These aren't just fleeting anxieties; they're deeply ingrained ways of thinking that distort our perception of ourselves and the world, hindering our progress toward healing and a fulfilling life. Imagine a fortress, its walls built brick by painful memory, each one reinforcing the others, making escape seem impossible. Breaking free requires a conscious, deliberate dismantling of these structures, one brick at a time.

Understanding the nature of these barriers is the first step. They manifest in many ways: self-doubt, crippling fear of failure, an inability to forgive oneself or others, and persistent negative self-talk, constantly undermining your efforts. These internal voices, echoing past hurts and criticisms, create a relentless internal conflict, draining your energy and preventing you from moving forward. They sabotage your attempts at self-compassion and make trusting others, even those who wish you well, incredibly difficult.

Consider the impact of learned helplessness, a state where repeated negative experiences lead to a belief that you lack control over your life. This can manifest as passivity in the face of challenges, a feeling of being trapped in a cycle of negativity. This sense of powerlessness is a significant mental barrier, making it difficult to even begin the healing process. You might find yourself avoiding situations that trigger anxiety, further isolating yourself and reinforcing the feeling of being trapped. Breaking free requires actively challenging this belief, identifying small areas where you can exert control and gradually building your sense of agency.

The process of overcoming these barriers is rarely straightforward. It's not a quick fix, but rather a gradual journey of self-discovery and growth. Expect setbacks. They are a normal part of the process. Don't let these setbacks discourage you; rather, view them as opportunities for learning and refinement. Celebrate your small victories and acknowledge the progress you're making, no matter how incremental it may seem. Each step forward, however small, is a testament to your strength and resilience.

One crucial strategy is to reframe your negative thoughts. When confronted with a negative thought, challenge its validity. Ask yourself: Is this thought truly accurate? Is there another way to interpret the situation? Often, negative thoughts are based on assumptions and distortions rather than objective reality. Replacing these with more balanced, realistic perspectives can significantly reduce their power over you. Journaling can be particularly helpful in identifying and challenging these ingrained thought patterns.

Cognitive Behavioral Therapy (CBT) provides a structured framework for this process. CBT techniques involve identifying and challenging negative thought patterns, replacing them with more constructive and realistic ones. This systematic approach can be incredibly effective in dismantling those mental barriers that stand in the way of your healing and well-being. It's about learning to manage your thoughts and emotions, not suppressing them. This empowers you to take control of your internal landscape.

Building self-compassion is another essential aspect of overcoming mental barriers. Treat yourself with the same kindness and understanding you would offer a friend struggling with similar challenges. Acknowledge your pain and suffering without judgment. Recognize that setbacks are a normal part of life, and that you are not defined by your mistakes or past experiences. Self-criticism only exacerbates the problem, creating a vicious cycle of negativity. Cultivate self-acceptance and celebrate your strengths and accomplishments, no matter how small they may seem.

Remember, the journey to healing is a marathon, not a sprint. It requires patience, persistence, and self-compassion. There will be days when you feel overwhelmed and discouraged. On these days, focus on self-care and reach out for support. Connecting with others who understand your struggles can provide invaluable comfort and encouragement. Don't hesitate to seek professional help; a therapist can provide guidance and support as you navigate this challenging but ultimately rewarding journey. Your healing is a testament to your courage and perseverance; celebrate the progress made, and continue the journey. The path to inner serenity is achievable, one step at a time.

3 Chapter 3: Seeking Solace

The journey from despair to solace isn't linear; it's a winding path, full of unexpected turns and moments of profound clarity. Sometimes, hope feels like a distant star, barely visible through the clouds of pain. Yet, even in the darkest hours, a tiny spark of hope persists. Nurture that spark. It might flicker, it might seem insignificant, but it holds the potential to ignite a powerful flame. Remember your strength. You've endured immense hardship, and that itself is a testament to your inner resilience. Acknowledge your past, but don't allow it to define your future. You are capable of so much more than you believe.

Finding solace often involves seeking guidance beyond oneself. Spiritual practices, whether religious or secular, offer a framework for understanding suffering and finding meaning in the face of adversity. Meditation, prayer, spending time in nature – these can provide a sense of peace and connection. Explore different spiritual paths and find what resonates with you. Don't feel pressured to conform to a particular belief system if it doesn't feel authentic. The core is finding something that brings you comfort and helps you connect with something larger than yourself. Remember that finding meaning isn't about suddenly understanding everything; it's about seeking understanding, and learning to accept life's uncertainties. Many find that this process of discovery strengthens their resilience significantly.

The power of human connection cannot be overstated. Surrounding yourself with supportive friends and family can provide a lifeline during difficult times. These individuals offer empathy, practical assistance, and a sense of belonging. Consider seeking out support groups or joining communities focused on shared experiences. This may include online forums or in-person meetings. Sharing your story with others who understand can be incredibly healing and empowering. It can ease the isolation often felt by those who have endured trauma, and help you build a network of caring individuals ready to lend support when needed.

Self-compassion is a fundamental aspect of the healing process. Treat yourself with the same kindness and understanding you would offer a dear friend who was going through similar challenges. Acknowledge your pain without judgment. Recognize that you're not alone in your struggle, and that your feelings are valid. Practice self-forgiveness. Release the guilt and shame that might be holding you back. Remember, healing is a journey, not a destination. There will be setbacks and moments of doubt, but with self-compassion, you can navigate these challenges with greater ease. Learning to treat yourself kindly, with empathy and understanding for your struggles, is as important as receiving external support. This approach greatly enhances the healing journey.

Building a life filled with serenity requires conscious effort and consistent practice. It's about cultivating gratitude for the good things in your life, both big and small. It's about learning to appreciate moments of joy and peace. It's also about setting realistic goals and celebrating your progress along the way. It is also about letting go of negative thoughts and feelings. It's about replacing them with feelings of acceptance and peace, by releasing the burden of past hurts and traumas. Remember this: focusing on the present moment can significantly reduce anxiety about the future and regrets about the past. Creating a serene and peaceful existence requires consistent work and self-awareness, but the benefits far outweigh the effort. You deserve to live a life filled with peace. You deserve to heal.

3.1 Finding Hope

Hope isn't a passive feeling; it's an active choice, a conscious decision to believe in a brighter future, even when the present feels overwhelmingly dark. It's about recognizing the strength you possess, the resilience you've already demonstrated in simply enduring what you have. You've survived; that's a monumental accomplishment, deserving of acknowledgement and celebration. Remember that strength, hold onto it tightly, because it is the bedrock upon which you will build your future.

Finding hope isn't about ignoring the pain; it's about acknowledging it, validating it, and then, gently, carefully, beginning to move forward. It's like navigating a treacherous mountain path; you wouldn't try to leap across the chasms; you'd find a sturdy, safe route, one step at a time. Similarly, healing isn't a race; there's no finish line where suddenly everything is perfect. It's a journey, and each small step forward is a victory.

Many find solace in spiritual practices. Prayer, meditation, or simply spending time in nature can provide a sense of peace and connection to something larger than themselves. For others, it's the connection with supportive friends and family that provides the essential lifeline. Identify your own sources of comfort. Is it through creative expression, like painting or writing?

Is it through physical activity, like yoga or a walk in the park? Whatever brings you a sense of calm and connection, nurture it. Make time for it; make it a priority.

Self-compassion is pivotal. Treat yourself with the same kindness and understanding you would offer a close friend in similar circumstances. Avoid self-criticism; instead, focus on self-encouragement. Recognize that setbacks are a natural part of the healing process, and they don't diminish your worth. You are worthy of love and compassion, regardless of your past experiences or present struggles. Remember this truth in the midst of challenges. You matter. Your experience matters. Your feelings matter.

Connecting with others who understand can be immensely powerful. Support groups, online forums, or even just conversations with trusted friends can offer a sense of belonging and shared experience. Knowing you're not alone in your struggles can significantly reduce feelings of isolation and shame. These connections can provide invaluable emotional support, sharing experiences and strategies for coping. This support is more than comfort; it's validation and the hope of navigating the path with others.

Consider professional help. Therapy offers a safe and confidential space to explore your trauma, develop coping mechanisms, and work towards healing. A therapist can provide guidance and support, helping you to process your emotions and develop healthy strategies for managing your challenges. It's not a sign of weakness; it's a sign of strength to seek professional help when you need it. Their expertise can offer support and strategies that may otherwise seem unreachable.

Hope is not the absence of fear or pain; it is the ability to live with them, to find meaning and purpose even amidst adversity. It's about acknowledging the darkness while simultaneously holding onto a vision of light. It is the unwavering belief in your capacity for growth, resilience, and ultimately, joy. Hope sustains us when all else feels lost, giving us strength to keep moving forward, one breath, one step, one day at a time.

Remember, healing is a marathon, not a sprint. There will be good days and bad days, moments of progress and moments of regression. Don't get discouraged by the setbacks; learn from them, and keep moving forward. The journey toward hope is unique to you. Trust your intuition, follow your heart, and know that you are capable of finding peace and healing. Your strength is remarkable. Your capacity for growth is immense. Believe in yourself and embrace the possibilities. Finding hope is not a destination, but a process, a journey of self-discovery and healing. It's a continuous process; even when serenity arrives, vigilance and self-care must continue. This isn't a race, it's a continuous process. You'll have ups and downs, which should be embraced for the growth they bring. The journey to finding hope is yours alone, a deeply personal journey of discovery. Trust your instincts, listen to your inner voice, and always remember your strength. You possess an incredible capacity for healing and growth. Embrace the journey, and the hope will find you.

3.2 Inner Strength

Drawing on your inner strength isn't about suddenly becoming superhuman; it's about cultivating a resilience built from the ground up, a quiet power that emerges from facing life's challenges head-on. It's about recognizing your inherent capabilities, even when obscured by adversity. This involves actively acknowledging your past experiences—the traumas, the losses, the heartbreaks—without letting them define who you are. Your past does not dictate your future. You are more than the sum of your struggles; you possess an untapped wellspring of strength waiting to be discovered.

Remember those moments where you felt utterly defeated, where hope seemed to dwindle? Recall how you persevered, even if you didn't fully comprehend your actions at the time. Those moments, those seemingly insignificant acts of defiance against despair, are testament to the enduring strength residing within you. This inner strength isn't something magically bestowed; it's cultivated, nurtured, and strengthened through conscious effort and self-awareness. You are the architect of your own resilience.

Start small. Notice the little victories, the daily acts of courage that might go unnoticed. Completing a challenging task, offering a helping hand, or simply overcoming a moment of self-doubt—these are all indicators of your inherent strength. Celebrate these achievements, no matter how seemingly insignificant they may seem. Acknowledge your efforts; you deserve recognition for your unwavering commitment to progress. Celebrate these small wins. They are stepping stones on your path to a stronger, more confident you.

Building inner strength necessitates self-compassion. Be kind to yourself, especially during moments of vulnerability and weakness. Treat yourself with the same understanding and empathy you would offer a close friend facing similar struggles. Self-criticism is a destructive force that weakens your resolve. Instead, practice self-forgiveness, acknowledging that mistakes are inevitable and learning from them is key. Your flaws are part of your story, not your definition. Accept yourself completely, flaws and all.

Cultivating mindfulness can significantly enhance your inner strength. Through practices like meditation and deep breathing, you learn to observe your thoughts and emotions without judgment. This detachment allows you to manage overwhelming feelings more effectively and respond to challenges with greater clarity. It's not about eliminating negative emotions, but rather learning to navigate them skillfully, understanding that they are temporary and do not dictate your overall well-being. Mindfulness helps you appreciate the present moment, grounding you in the now and lessening the power of past traumas or future anxieties.

Connecting with others forms a powerful support system that bolsters your inner strength. Sharing your experiences with trusted friends, family, or a therapist can alleviate feelings of isolation and provide a sense of validation. This shared experience fosters a sense of belonging and reminds you that you are not alone in your struggles. These connections provide emotional support, encouragement, and practical advice, contributing significantly to your resilience and sense of self-worth. Don't underestimate the power of human connection.

Forgiveness, both of yourself and others, plays a critical role in strengthening your inner core. Holding onto anger and resentment only serves to weigh you down, hindering your ability to move forward and embrace a healthier future. Forgiveness isn't about condoning harmful actions, but rather about releasing the emotional burden that keeps you tethered to the past. This process can be challenging, requiring time and self-reflection. Consider journaling as a tool for exploring and processing your feelings, and seeking professional guidance if needed. Your healing journey deserves your utmost care and attention. The power of forgiveness is transformative.

Finally, remember that building inner strength is a continuous process, a journey of self-discovery and growth. There will be setbacks and challenges along the way, but these are opportunities for learning and further development. Embrace the challenges, view them as opportunities to test your resilience, and learn from every experience. Your inner strength will only continue to grow stronger with each hurdle you overcome. Each experience, whether positive or negative, contributes to your personal evolution. The journey of building inner strength is a lifetime commitment, but the rewards are immense.

3.3 Spiritual Guidance

Spiritual guidance, in its broadest sense, isn't about adhering to a specific religion; it's about connecting with something larger than yourself—a source of comfort, strength, and meaning. This connection can manifest in countless ways, from prayer and meditation to spending time in nature or engaging in creative pursuits. The key is to find what resonates deeply with your soul, what helps you feel grounded and centered amidst the chaos. This inner compass will guide you toward healing, allowing you to confront the shadows of your past and embrace a brighter future.

For some, this might involve formal religious practices, finding solace and strength in communal worship, shared rituals, and the guidance of spiritual leaders. The sense of belonging and shared purpose can be incredibly powerful, offering a sense of community and unwavering support. This shared experience, this collective strength, can help individuals navigate challenging periods and feel less alone in their struggle. Others may find solace in a solitary practice, in silent contemplation and introspection.

Perhaps your spiritual path unfolds through the quiet beauty of nature. The rhythmic crash of ocean waves, the serene stillness of a forest, the vast expanse of a starlit sky—these experiences can be profoundly calming, fostering a deep connection with the natural world and a sense of awe and wonder. Nature's ability to offer peace and perspective is invaluable, serving as a constant reminder of the larger forces at play and our place within them. This can provide a sense of grounding and stability, allowing for reflection and emotional processing.

For others, creativity might be the key. Expressing yourself through art, music, writing, or any other creative outlet can be a powerful form of self-discovery and healing. Through creative expression, emotions find an outlet, buried feelings surface, and a sense of purpose emerges. This process allows for a deeper understanding of oneself and the ability to process trauma in a healthy way. The act of creation itself can be a meditative practice, a journey of self-exploration leading to inner peace.

Finding your spiritual path is a deeply personal journey, a unique exploration of your inner landscape. There's no right or wrong way to connect with your spirituality, no single method guaranteed to work for everyone. Experiment, explore, and trust your intuition. Be open to new experiences and perspectives. Allow yourself to be guided by your inner voice, that quiet whisper that knows what your soul truly needs.

Remember, this isn't about finding a quick fix or a magical solution to your problems. It's about cultivating a relationship with your inner self, developing a deeper understanding of your values, and finding a sense of meaning and purpose in your life. It's about building resilience, fostering self-compassion, and creating a life aligned with your deepest values. Your spiritual journey is a lifelong process, a continuous exploration of self, a constant unfolding of your potential. It is a journey of growth and healing, a movement towards a more peaceful and fulfilling life.

Ultimately, spiritual guidance is about finding a source of strength and inspiration that helps you navigate life's challenges with grace and resilience. It's about cultivating inner peace and creating a life that is meaningful and fulfilling. It's about fostering a deep connection with yourself and the world around you. The journey may be challenging at times, but the rewards—a sense of purpose, inner peace, and deep connection—are well worth the effort. It's a process of self-discovery, not a destination, and it requires patience, self-awareness and a willingness to explore various paths. The beauty lies in the exploration itself, the continuous growth and evolution of self.

The path to spiritual healing is often paved with unexpected turns, requiring flexibility, perseverance, and a willingness to embrace uncertainty. Don't be afraid to explore different approaches, to try new things, and to discover what works best for you. Remember that setbacks are a natural part of the process; they are opportunities for learning and growth. Keep moving forward, even when the journey feels difficult. Believe in your ability to heal and to find your own unique path to inner peace.

And finally, remember that you are not alone on this journey. There are countless people who have walked similar paths, who understand your struggles and your triumphs. Seek out support from friends, family, or a spiritual community. Allow yourself to be vulnerable and to share your experiences. The support and understanding of others can make all the difference in the world. Embrace the power of human connection and allow others to help support you on this important journey. You are stronger than you think, and the path to inner serenity is within your reach.

3.4 Community Support

Finding solace isn't always a solitary journey. It's often in the shared experiences, the understanding glances, and the collective strength of a community that true healing begins. Connecting with others who understand your struggles can be incredibly validating and empowering, a powerful antidote to the isolating effects of trauma. This shared understanding transcends mere words; it's felt in the unspoken empathy, the shared tears, and the quiet moments of mutual recognition. This isn't about weakness; it's about leveraging the strength inherent in human connection.

Support groups, whether online or in-person, offer a safe space for vulnerability. Sharing your story, hearing others' experiences, and realizing you're not alone can be profoundly transformative. This isn't about seeking pity; it's about finding strength in shared experience. The mutual support fosters a sense of belonging and shared purpose, turning a potentially isolating experience into a collective journey of healing. The sense of community builds resilience, making it easier to confront challenges.

Think of it like this: imagine a single tree battling a storm. It might withstand some gusts, but the chances of it surviving unscathed are slim. Now, imagine a forest. Those same winds might cause some damage, but the collective strength of the trees, their interlocked roots, and their mutual support greatly increases their chances of survival. We are, in essence, a forest of individuals.

Finding the right community can take time. Don't get discouraged if the first group you try doesn't feel like the right fit. Keep searching. Consider your specific needs and the type of support you're looking for. Some groups are focused on specific traumas, while others provide broader support for mental health challenges. Online forums offer anonymity and accessibility, whereas in-person groups provide face-to-face interaction.

Remember, these aren't just groups; they're networks of people who truly understand. They offer practical advice, coping strategies learned through shared experience, and a listening ear during moments of despair. They can help you navigate bureaucratic hurdles, provide resources, and even simply offer a warm, comforting presence. The emotional support is vital, providing a buffer against the overwhelming feelings that often accompany trauma. Don't underestimate the power of shared laughter, which can be as therapeutic as shared tears.

It's crucial to approach community support with an open mind and a willingness to participate. It's a two-way street. While you receive support, you also contribute to the collective strength of the group. Your experience can help others, and your participation builds a stronger sense of community for everyone involved. Sharing your story, even if it feels difficult, can be deeply healing for both you and those who listen.

Beyond formal support groups, remember the power of informal connections. Lean on trusted friends and family. They may not fully understand the complexities of your trauma, but their love and support can provide invaluable comfort and strength. Cultivate these relationships; nurture them and let them be a source of resilience. This might involve expressing your needs clearly, setting boundaries, and actively participating in building these bonds.

Don't be afraid to seek professional guidance in addition to community support. A therapist can provide a safe and structured environment to process trauma, equip you with specific coping mechanisms, and help you navigate challenging emotions. Therapy complements community support; it's not a replacement. It provides individualized support, and a deeper dive into your personal experience, all while working alongside the support you draw from your community.

Your healing journey is unique. Finding the right balance of professional help, community support, and self-care is key. Be patient with yourself, celebrate small victories, and remember that even in the darkest moments, there is strength to be found in connection. The path to serenity is a winding one, and a supportive community can help guide you along the way. Embrace the journey, and allow your community to embrace you in return.

3.5 Self-Compassion

Self-compassion isn't selfish; it's essential. It's about treating yourself with the same kindness, understanding, and concern you'd offer a dear friend struggling with similar challenges.

Imagine a friend confessing their failures; you wouldn't berate them, would you? You'd likely offer support, reminding them of their strengths and inherent worth. That's the essence of self-compassion—extending that same grace to yourself.

Many of us, especially after experiencing significant hardship, develop a harsh inner critic. This voice relentlessly judges our shortcomings, magnifying our mistakes, and leaving us feeling inadequate. This critical self-talk is often rooted in past trauma, societal pressures, or even perfectionistic tendencies. It fuels negative self-perception and undermines our ability to cope with life's inevitable setbacks. Breaking free from this cycle demands conscious effort, a deliberate shift in perspective.

Practicing self-compassion involves three core components: self-kindness, common humanity, and mindfulness. Self-kindness replaces self-judgment with self-understanding and acceptance. Instead of criticizing your flaws, acknowledge your imperfections with empathy. Recognize that everyone makes mistakes; you are not alone in your struggles. Remember that being human means being imperfect.

Common humanity reminds you that suffering and imperfection are part of the shared human experience. No one is immune to setbacks, pain, or failure. Connecting with this shared human experience diminishes feelings of isolation and shame. It normalizes your struggles, placing them within the broader context of the human condition. This realization helps to counter the tendency to isolate yourself in your pain, believing you're uniquely flawed or deficient.

Mindfulness involves paying attention to your thoughts and emotions without judgment. It's about observing your inner critic without engaging with its negativity. When you notice self-critical thoughts arising, simply acknowledge them without getting swept away by their intensity. Mindfulness allows you to create a space between yourself and your thoughts, creating the emotional distance needed to respond with compassion rather than judgment.

One practical technique is the "self-compassion break." When you're feeling overwhelmed by negative emotions, take a few moments to pause. Put your hand on your heart, or on a part of your body that feels especially tense, and gently repeat a self-compassionate phrase to yourself—something like, "This is a difficult moment, but it will pass," or "May I be kind to myself." The simple act of placing your hand on your heart can be remarkably grounding and soothing.

Consider journaling to explore your inner critic's voice. Write down the critical thoughts that arise throughout your day. Analyze them, question their validity, and challenge their negativity.

Instead of accepting these thoughts as truth, begin to reframe them with more compassion and understanding. For instance, if you're beating yourself up for a mistake, ask: "What would I say to a friend in this situation?" Your response will likely be much gentler than your inner critic's judgment.

Remember, self-compassion is a skill, not a personality trait. It requires practice and patience. There will be times when self-criticism resurfaces; that's completely normal. The key is to treat these moments as opportunities for growth, as chances to practice self-kindness and redirect your focus towards self-compassion. Don't be discouraged by setbacks; embrace them as part of the ongoing learning process.

Begin by incorporating small acts of self-compassion into your daily routine. Engage in activities you enjoy, even if it's just for a few minutes each day. Listen to your body's needs, and prioritize rest and relaxation. Be mindful of your self-talk, challenging negative thoughts and replacing them with self-affirming statements. These small changes, consistently practiced, can significantly impact your overall well-being and cultivate a greater sense of self-acceptance and peace. The journey to self-compassion is a journey of self-discovery and healing, a journey worth undertaking. The rewards are immeasurable: reduced stress, improved emotional regulation, increased resilience, and a deeper sense of self-worth. It's an investment in your well-being—an investment you deserve.

4 Chapter 4: Paths to Healing

Many find solace in professional therapy. It provides a safe space to explore deeply rooted issues, a structured environment for processing trauma, and the guidance of a trained professional. A therapist can help you understand the underlying mechanisms of your emotional responses, develop coping strategies tailored to your unique experiences, and work through the complex feelings that may feel overwhelming alone. Remember, seeking professional help is a sign of strength, not weakness. This journey is about reclaiming your life, and a therapist can be your invaluable guide. Effective therapeutic techniques, like Cognitive Behavioral Therapy (CBT) or Trauma-Focused Cognitive Behavioral Therapy (TF-CBT), can offer powerful tools for managing symptoms and fostering emotional resilience. These approaches focus on identifying and modifying negative thought patterns and behaviors, empowering you to take control of your emotional landscape.

Mindfulness practices offer a powerful pathway to healing. These techniques, rooted in ancient wisdom, emphasize present moment awareness. By focusing on your breath, body sensations, and the immediate environment, you can gently detach from overwhelming thoughts and emotions. Meditation, even in short bursts, can help calm your nervous system, reducing feelings of anxiety and promoting a sense of inner peace. Mindfulness practices aren't about emptying your mind; they're about cultivating a non-judgmental observation of your thoughts and feelings. This awareness is key to breaking free from negative thought cycles and fostering emotional regulation. Start with simple guided meditations, and gradually increase your practice time as you feel more comfortable. Mindful movement practices like yoga or Tai Chi can also enhance the benefits, combining physical activity with mental focus.

Engaging in self-compassion is a critical element of your healing journey. This involves treating yourself with the same kindness, understanding, and patience that you would offer a close friend facing similar challenges. Recognize that you're not alone in your struggles and that everyone experiences setbacks and imperfections. Acknowledge your pain, rather than judging or criticizing yourself for feeling it. Self-compassion is not self-indulgence, but a powerful antidote to self-criticism. It fosters resilience, allowing you to approach challenges with renewed strength. Remember that healing takes time, and it's okay to have ups and downs along the way. Be gentle with yourself, offering encouragement and understanding, rather than harsh self-judgment.

Journaling can be an incredibly helpful tool, offering a private space to process your emotions. Write freely, without editing or censoring your thoughts and feelings. Allowing yourself to express your emotions unburdened can be remarkably cathartic. You might find that simply putting your thoughts on paper helps clarify your feelings and create emotional distance from overwhelming experiences. Don't be afraid to explore your past experiences, your present challenges, and your hopes for the future. Journaling isn't a therapeutic substitute, but rather a powerful tool for self-reflection that can enhance your therapeutic work. It's a unique way to build your emotional awareness and understanding of the healing process.

Learning to forgive – yourself and others – is an essential step toward healing. Holding onto resentment and anger consumes your energy and prevents you from moving forward. Forgiveness is not about condoning harmful behavior, but about freeing yourself from the burden of carrying the pain. It's a process, not a single event; it involves acknowledging the hurt, accepting your feelings, and releasing the negative emotions that bind you to the past. Consider the benefits of letting go – regaining emotional freedom, reducing stress and anxiety, and creating space for personal growth. You are not required to forgive instantaneously; it's a journey, not a race. This process takes time and self-compassion.

Exploring creative outlets can be surprisingly therapeutic. Whether it's painting, writing, playing music, or engaging in any other creative activity that resonates with you, the process of creation can be a profound form of self-expression. It provides an outlet for emotions that may be difficult to articulate verbally. Through creative expression, you can process your experiences, understand your emotions, and gain insight into yourself in a safe and expressive manner. There is no need for artistic talent; the value lies in the creative process itself. Allow yourself to explore different mediums and find what resonates most deeply with your soul. Express yourself without judgment and allow your creative energy to flow.

4.1 Therapy's Embrace

Therapy offers a structured path through the tangled undergrowth of your past. It provides a safe space, a contained environment where you can unpack the burdens you carry, examine them piece by piece, and begin to understand their impact. This isn't about erasing the past; it's about integrating it into your present in a way that doesn't control your future. Remember, you're not alone in this; many have walked similar roads.

Finding the right therapist is crucial. It's like finding the right key to unlock a door. Consider your comfort level; do you prefer someone older or younger? Male or female? Someone with a specific expertise, perhaps someone specializing in trauma-informed care, if that aligns with your needs? Don't settle for a therapist you don't connect with; the therapeutic relationship is foundational. Trust your gut.

The therapeutic process isn't a quick fix; it's a journey, a gradual unfolding. Expect ups and downs, moments of breakthrough interwoven with periods of stagnation. Be patient with yourself. Progress is rarely linear. Celebrate small victories, acknowledge setbacks, and remember that consistency is key. Just as a muscle strengthens with regular exercise, your emotional resilience will grow stronger over time.

Therapy provides tools to navigate challenging emotions. You'll learn techniques like cognitive behavioral therapy (CBT), which helps to identify and challenge negative thought patterns, and dialectical behavior therapy (DBT), which equips you with skills to manage intense emotions and improve relationships. These are not magic wands; they are practical strategies, requiring commitment and practice to integrate effectively into your daily life. Think of them as your personal toolkit for emotional well-being.

Remember, therapy isn't just about dealing with the past; it's about building a stronger, healthier future. It's about learning to regulate your emotions, build healthier relationships, and develop a more compassionate understanding of yourself. It's about reclaiming your narrative and rewriting your story, a story where you are the author, empowered to shape your own destiny. This is your opportunity to heal, not just from the past traumas, but to grow into a stronger, more resilient self.

One powerful aspect of therapy is the exploration of self-compassion. Many of us are our own harshest critics, judging ourselves relentlessly for past mistakes and perceived failures. Therapy offers a space to challenge this self-criticism, to foster self-acceptance and kindness. Learn to treat yourself with the same empathy and understanding you would offer a close friend struggling with similar challenges. This is a powerful tool for emotional healing and personal growth.

The therapeutic relationship, itself, can be a powerful source of healing. The consistent support and understanding of a trained professional provides a sense of security and validation that many have lacked in their lives. This consistent presence, this unwavering support, can be invaluable in navigating difficult emotions and building self-esteem. Your therapist is there to guide you, not to judge you. Their role is to help you understand yourself better and build a path forward.

Remember that your participation is key to the success of therapy. It's a collaborative effort; it's a partnership where you and your therapist work together to achieve your therapeutic goals. Be open, honest, and proactive in your sessions. Ask questions, share your concerns, and don't hesitate to express your needs. Your therapist is there to help you, but only you can fully determine the course of your healing journey. This is your journey; take the reins and shape it into something that resonates deeply with who you are becoming.

Effective therapy often involves homework. This might involve journaling, practicing specific techniques learned in session, or engaging in activities designed to promote self-reflection. This isn't extra work; it's an investment in your well-being. By actively engaging in these activities, you strengthen the work done in sessions, and accelerate your progress toward healing. Think of it as strengthening your emotional muscles to build a better, healthier you.

Finally, recognize that therapy is a deeply personal journey. There is no one-size-fits-all approach. What works for one person may not work for another. Be open to exploring different therapeutic modalities, and don't be afraid to seek a second opinion if necessary. Trust your instincts and remember that your healing journey is unique to you, and its success depends on your active participation and your commitment to your own well-being. Take this opportunity to build a life filled with serenity, resilience, and self-acceptance.

4.2 Mindfulness Practices

Mindfulness, at its core, is about paying attention to the present moment without judgment. It's not about emptying your mind, a misconception many beginners hold, but rather about observing your thoughts, feelings, and sensations as they arise, acknowledging them without getting swept away. This non-reactive observation is key; it allows you to create space between yourself and your emotional turmoil, breaking the cycle of reactivity that often fuels anxiety and distress. Imagine watching clouds drift across the sky—you notice them, acknowledge their presence, but you don't try to control their movement. That's the essence of mindful observation.

Begin with short, manageable periods of mindfulness practice. Even five minutes a day can yield significant benefits. Find a quiet space where you can sit comfortably. Close your eyes gently, or keep them softly focused on a single point. Bring your attention to your breath, noticing the sensation of the air entering and leaving your nostrils, the rise and fall of your chest or abdomen. When your mind wanders—and it inevitably will—gently redirect your attention back to your breath. Don't berate yourself for getting distracted; simply acknowledge the distraction and return to your focus. This is a skill you're developing, and like any skill, it requires patience and consistent practice.

One effective mindfulness technique is body scan meditation. This involves bringing your awareness systematically through different parts of your body, noticing any sensations without judgment. Start with your toes, paying attention to any tingling, warmth, or pressure. Slowly move your awareness up your body, noticing sensations in your feet, ankles, calves, and so on, all the way to the top of your head. Again, the key is to simply observe without judgment; you might find some areas tense, others relaxed. Simply acknowledge these sensations without trying to change them. This practice enhances body awareness and can help you identify physical manifestations of stress and anxiety, allowing you to address them more effectively.

Incorporating mindfulness into your daily life can be surprisingly simple. While you're eating, for example, pay close attention to the taste, texture, and smell of your food. Engage all your senses fully; notice the colors, the temperature. This mindful eating practice can transform a mundane activity into a moment of presence and appreciation. Similarly, when you're walking, focus on the sensation of your feet on the ground, the rhythm of your steps, the feeling of the wind on your skin. Even seemingly insignificant actions, when approached mindfully, can become opportunities for connection with the present moment and a release from rumination on the past or anxiety about the future.

Remember, mindfulness isn't a quick fix. It's a journey, not a destination. There will be days when you find it challenging to stay present, days when your mind feels like a whirlwind of thoughts. These moments are opportunities for self-compassion, not for self-criticism. Treat yourself with the same kindness and understanding you would offer a friend struggling with similar challenges. Acknowledge your difficulties, accept them without judgment, and gently guide your attention back to the present. This is crucial. Consistent effort over time is what yields meaningful results. Regular practice, even in small increments, is far more valuable than sporadic attempts at intense mindfulness sessions.

Cultivating mindfulness is not merely a tool for managing stress and anxiety. It's a pathway to deeper self-understanding and compassionate self-acceptance. By observing your thoughts and emotions without judgment, you begin to develop a more nuanced understanding of your inner world. This self-awareness allows you to identify patterns of thought and behavior that may be contributing to your suffering and to make conscious choices to alter those patterns. Mindfulness becomes a form of self-inquiry, helping you unravel the complexities of your emotional landscape.

Furthermore, mindfulness practices can significantly enhance your relationships. When you're fully present with someone, you're better able to listen deeply, empathize genuinely, and connect authentically. Rather than reacting defensively to their words or actions, you can choose to respond with understanding and compassion, improving communication and fostering stronger bonds. This is particularly valuable in the context of trauma recovery, where rebuilding trust and fostering healthy relationships is crucial.

Beyond the immediate benefits of stress reduction and emotional regulation, mindfulness cultivates a sense of inner peace and resilience. By consistently practicing mindfulness, you develop a greater capacity to handle life's inevitable challenges with equanimity and grace. You're better equipped to navigate difficult situations without being overwhelmed by negative emotions, and you develop a stronger sense of inner strength and self-reliance. This inner resilience enables you to weather life's storms with greater composure and emerge stronger on the other side. It's a lifelong practice, continuously evolving and refining itself as you grow and change.

Finally, integrate mindfulness into your routine gradually, rather than trying to overhaul your life overnight. Start with small, manageable steps and celebrate your progress along the way. Don't get discouraged by setbacks; they are a natural part of the process. Remember to be kind to yourself, especially during moments of frustration or self-doubt. Your journey towards inner serenity is a personal one, and progress will be unique to you. Embrace the journey, and appreciate the small victories along the way. This mindful approach extends even to your practice of mindfulness itself. Observe your progress without judgment and recognize your growth, no matter how seemingly small. The journey of self-discovery through mindfulness is a long and rewarding one.

5 Chapter 5: Rediscovering Self

Rediscovering yourself after profound trauma isn't a linear journey; it's a winding path, filled with unexpected detours and moments of breathtaking clarity. It begins with acknowledging the depth of your wounds, understanding that the scars you carry are testaments to your resilience, not your weakness. It's about accepting that healing isn't about erasing the past, but integrating it into a richer, more nuanced understanding of who you are.

Forgiveness, often mistakenly viewed as condoning the actions of others, is actually a powerful act of self-liberation. It doesn't mean forgetting or minimizing the pain inflicted; instead, it means releasing the grip of resentment and anger that continues to hold you captive. It's a release of the emotional energy you've been expending on the past, freeing you to invest that energy in yourself and your future. Picture it like this: a heavy weight you've carried for years is finally lifted, allowing you to stand taller, to breathe deeper, to move forward with renewed lightness and strength.

Self-acceptance, a cornerstone of this rediscovery, is about embracing your imperfections, your flaws, and your vulnerabilities. It's recognizing that these aspects of yourself are not things to be hidden or ashamed of, but integral parts of your unique story. It's recognizing your worth, your innate value, irrespective of external validation. Stop comparing yourself to others, and start celebrating your own authentic self, quirks and all. This isn't about self-indulgence; it's about self-compassion, nurturing yourself with the same kindness and understanding you would offer a dear friend.

Finding renewed purpose involves identifying your passions, rekindling dormant interests, or discovering new ones entirely. This is not necessarily about grand gestures or life-altering decisions; it can be as simple as reconnecting with an old hobby, volunteering your time to a cause you believe in, or learning a new skill that ignites your curiosity. The key is to engage in activities that bring you joy, that tap into your creativity and potential, that allow you to contribute something meaningful to the world. This renewed sense of purpose will invigorate you, providing a sense of direction and fulfillment.

Personal growth is a continuous process, a journey of self-discovery that never truly ends. It's about consciously seeking out new experiences, challenging your limiting beliefs, and stepping outside of your comfort zone. This might involve pursuing further education, traveling to new places, engaging in meaningful conversations with others, or simply reflecting on your experiences and learning from your mistakes. It's about continually expanding your awareness, deepening your understanding of yourself and the world around you, and cultivating a sense of inner peace and contentment. It's the act of actively shaping your future, rather than passively accepting what comes your way. This active participation in your own growth is crucial for building resilience and a fulfilling life. Remember, you are not defined by your past traumas; your story is still being written, and you have the power to shape its ending.

Embrace the journey, for it is in the process of rediscovery that true healing occurs. The path to self-acceptance and renewed purpose may be challenging at times, demanding patience, perseverance, and self-compassion. But know this: the rewards far outweigh the challenges. The journey of rediscovering yourself is a journey of empowerment, a journey of reclaiming your life, your strength, and your inherent worth. It's a journey that will lead you to a place of serenity, a place where you can finally live a life filled with joy, purpose, and lasting peace. The ultimate destination is a self you'll love and respect deeply, a self finally free from the shadows of the past. This is the true essence of healing and the foundation for a truly fulfilling life. Trust in your journey, your strength, and your ability to heal. You deserve this peace. You deserve this rediscovery.

5.1 Embracing Imperfection

We all strive for perfection, a flawless image reflecting back at us from the mirror of life. But what happens when that mirror shatters, revealing not the flawless reflection we anticipated, but a mosaic of cracks and imperfections? This is not a failure; it's the reality of the human experience. Embracing these imperfections, these cracks in our carefully constructed facades, is the key to unlocking a deeper, more authentic sense of self. It's about accepting the messy, complicated, and sometimes downright ugly parts of ourselves—the parts we often hide from the world and, even more critically, from ourselves.

The journey toward self-acceptance isn't a sprint; it's a marathon, a winding path filled with unexpected detours and occasional setbacks. There will be days when you stumble, when the weight of your imperfections feels overwhelming, threatening to drag you back down into the darkness of self-doubt. This is normal. It's part of the process. Don't judge yourself for these moments of weakness; instead, acknowledge them, learn from them, and move forward with renewed determination. Remember, progress, not perfection, is the ultimate goal.

It's easy to get caught up in comparisons, to constantly measure ourselves against others. Social media, especially, can exacerbate this, creating a distorted reality where everyone seems to be living a flawless, picture-perfect life. But remember that these curated online personas rarely reflect the whole truth. They are carefully constructed illusions, carefully crafted to project an image of success and happiness that simply isn't achievable in real life. Focus on your own journey, your own progress, and your own unique strengths.

Forgiveness plays a crucial role in embracing imperfection. It's not just about forgiving others; it's about forgiving yourself. We all make mistakes, we all experience setbacks, and we all fall short of our own expectations at times. To hold onto these mistakes, these imperfections, is to carry a heavy burden. Forgiveness is about letting go of that burden, freeing yourself from the shackles of self-criticism and allowing yourself to move forward with a lighter heart and a clearer mind. It's about extending compassion to yourself, just as you would to a loved one facing similar struggles.

Self-compassion is not self-indulgence; it's a powerful tool for navigating life's inevitable challenges. Treat yourself with the same kindness, understanding, and patience that you would offer a close friend. When faced with setbacks, don't beat yourself up; instead, offer yourself words of encouragement and support. Acknowledge your feelings without judgment. Remember that everyone makes mistakes, and that imperfections are a natural part of the human experience. These moments of self-compassion are not signs of weakness, but acts of strength. They demonstrate self-awareness and a willingness to acknowledge our vulnerability—two key components of healing.

Rediscovering your worth and embracing your imperfections doesn't happen overnight. It takes courage, self-reflection, and a deep commitment to personal growth. This is not merely about accepting what is; it's about actively choosing to love the person you are, flaws and all. The path to self-acceptance isn't linear. There will be peaks and valleys, times of great progress and times of stagnation. Be patient with yourself and persistent in your efforts. Remember that progress, not perfection, is the true measure of success in this journey.

This process of embracing imperfection extends beyond self-acceptance. It informs the way we interact with others, fostering empathy, understanding, and compassion. When we are comfortable with our own imperfections, we become more accepting of the imperfections in others. This creates a ripple effect of kindness, allowing for deeper, more meaningful connections with those around us. It builds a strong foundation for healthy, resilient relationships, relationships built on authenticity rather than the unattainable ideal of perfection. Such relationships are more tolerant and forgiving, fostering a sense of belonging and support during challenging times.

In essence, embracing imperfection is not about lowering your standards; it's about shifting your perspective. It's about recognizing that your worth isn't determined by your flaws, but by your resilience, your capacity for growth, and your ability to find beauty in the unexpected. It's about celebrating your unique qualities, your individuality, and your remarkable ability to navigate life's complexities. This acceptance paves the way for a life lived with greater authenticity, deeper self-understanding, and profound contentment. It's about finding serenity not in the pursuit of a flawless existence, but in the acceptance of a beautifully imperfect one.

5.2 Forgiveness's Power

Forgiveness isn't about condoning the actions of others; it's about releasing yourself from the prison of resentment. Holding onto anger, bitterness, and pain only serves to further injure you, keeping you chained to the past. It's a heavy burden, weighing down your spirit and hindering your ability to move forward. Imagine carrying a sack of rocks – each rock representing a hurtful memory, a betrayal, a wrong. Eventually, that sack becomes unbearable, crushing you under its weight. Forgiveness is about setting down that sack, freeing yourself from its oppressive weight. It's about choosing peace over pain.

Forgiving someone, even yourself, doesn't mean forgetting what happened. It's not about minimizing the hurt you've endured; it's about choosing to no longer let that hurt dictate your present and future. It's a conscious decision to prioritize your own well-being, acknowledging the past while refusing to be a prisoner of it. Remember the vivid detail of a sun-drenched meadow, the warmth on your skin – that's the feeling you should aim to cultivate within yourself. Letting go doesn't erase the past; it allows you to see it with fresh eyes, to understand it without being consumed by it. It's the crucial transition from victimhood to empowerment.

The process of forgiveness can be challenging, a journey fraught with emotional ups and downs. You might find yourself oscillating between moments of understanding and surges of anger. It's not a linear progression; some days will feel easier than others. Allow yourself the time and space to feel whatever arises without judgment. Don't suppress your emotions; acknowledge them. Journaling, meditation, or talking to a trusted friend or therapist can help you process these feelings effectively. Each step toward understanding and compassion is a victory, a demonstration of your strength and resilience.

Self-forgiveness often proves even more challenging than forgiving others. We are often our harshest critics, holding ourselves to impossible standards. Mistakes are inevitable; they are part of the human experience. Learn to accept your imperfections, acknowledging your role in past events without dwelling on self-blame. This doesn't equate to self-indulgence, but rather a recognition of our shared humanity. Remember that every mistake is an opportunity to learn and grow, to choose a different path in the future. Self-compassion is the cornerstone of self-forgiveness, allowing you to move forward without the crippling weight of self-recrimination. Embrace your flaws, for they are integral to your unique narrative.

Forgiving others isn't about them; it's about you. It's about reclaiming your power, freeing yourself from the constraints of resentment. When you hold onto anger, you allow the past to control your present. Forgiveness is a choice, a conscious decision to break free from that cycle and to create space for healing and joy. It empowers you to redefine your relationship with your past, transforming it from a source of pain into a source of wisdom and personal growth. It's a path that allows you to create a more authentic, more joyful life. Consider this: the sun rises each day regardless of the darkness of the night, and so too will the light of forgiveness illuminate your path forward.

The path to forgiveness may be winding and filled with obstacles, but the destination – a life lived with serenity and peace – is worth the journey. It is a testament to the human spirit's capacity for resilience, healing, and transformation. It's about rediscovering your inner strength and recognizing the boundless potential within yourself. Forgiveness isn't a sign of weakness; it's a profound act of courage, a testament to your capacity for growth and self-love. It's about understanding that holding onto anger only perpetuates suffering. It is the freedom to embrace a future unburdened by the past. It's about the release of past pain, finally giving you the power to write your future. This is your opportunity to heal.

5.3 Self-Acceptance

Self-acceptance isn't about magically erasing past hurts; it's about acknowledging them, understanding their impact, and choosing to move forward. It's a process, not a destination, a continuous journey of self-discovery and growth. It's about recognizing that your past experiences, while shaping you, don't define you. You are more than the sum of your struggles. You possess strengths, resilience, and an inherent worth that deserves acknowledgment, even when feelings of inadequacy linger.

Learning to embrace imperfection is key. Perfection is an illusion, a unattainable standard that sets us up for constant disappointment. We all make mistakes, we all have flaws. These imperfections are not weaknesses; they're what make us unique and human. Trying to hide or deny them only fuels self-criticism and prevents genuine self-acceptance. Instead, acknowledge your flaws with kindness and understanding, recognizing that they are simply part of your story. Learn from them, grow from them, but don't let them diminish your sense of self-worth.

Forgiveness plays a critical role. This doesn't mean condoning harmful actions; rather, it's about releasing the anger, resentment, and pain that hold you captive. Holding onto these negative emotions only hurts you, prolonging the suffering and hindering your ability to move forward. Forgiveness, first and foremost, is for yourself. It's about freeing yourself from the burden of carrying past hurts, allowing yourself to heal and to make space for peace. It may require time and effort, perhaps even professional guidance, but the eventual release is profoundly liberating.

Self-compassion is the heart of self-acceptance. Treat yourself with the same kindness, understanding, and empathy you would offer a close friend struggling with similar challenges. Challenge negative self-talk; replace harsh judgments with supportive affirmations. Remind yourself that everyone makes mistakes, and that setbacks are opportunities for growth. Practice self-soothing techniques, like deep breathing exercises or spending time in nature, to nurture your emotional well-being. Engage in activities that bring you joy and fulfillment; prioritize self-care. These acts of self-compassion reinforce your inherent worth and pave the way for true self-acceptance.

Rediscovering your purpose is intrinsically linked to self-acceptance. When we truly accept ourselves, we're better equipped to identify our values, passions, and goals. This isn't about finding some grand life mission; it's about aligning your actions with your authentic self. What brings you meaning? What activities make you feel alive and engaged? Exploring these questions can help you discover a sense of purpose that fuels your motivation and strengthens your self-belief. This purpose might evolve over time; what matters is that it feels genuine and reflects your values.

Personal growth is an ongoing process of self-discovery and development, not a one-time event. Embrace the opportunity for continued learning and self-improvement. Seek out new experiences, challenge yourself, and step outside your comfort zone. This continuous expansion of your horizons fosters self-awareness and strengthens your sense of self. Be patient and kind to yourself throughout this journey; remember that progress, not perfection, is the goal. It's about consistent effort, not immediate transformation. Celebrate small victories and learn from setbacks, and keep moving forward. The path to self-acceptance is a marathon, not a sprint, and the rewards are immeasurable. The journey may be challenging, but it is ultimately one of profound self-discovery and liberation. Embrace the process, trust in your inherent worth, and celebrate the extraordinary individual you are. Your journey toward self-acceptance is a testament to your resilience and inner strength.

5.4 Renewed Purpose

Finding renewed purpose isn't about magically erasing the past; it's about consciously choosing a new direction, a path forward illuminated by the lessons learned, not defined by the pain endured. It's a powerful act of self-creation, a testament to your resilience and inner strength. This process is deeply personal, a journey unique to each individual, yet some common threads weave through the tapestry of recovery.

For many, the search begins with acknowledging the past without being consumed by it. It's a delicate balance – honoring the experiences that shaped you without letting them dictate your future. This means actively choosing to focus your energy on what you can control, on building a future that feels authentic and fulfilling. This isn't about forgetting; it's about reframing, seeing the past not as a prison but as a springboard for growth. It requires courage, a willingness to confront difficult emotions, and unwavering self-belief.

Self-compassion becomes your ally in this journey. Treat yourself with the same kindness and understanding you would offer a dear friend struggling with similar challenges. Remember, healing isn't linear. There will be setbacks, moments of doubt, and times when the weight of the past feels overwhelming. These are not failures but opportunities for growth, chances to practice self-compassion, to reaffirm your commitment to healing and building a better future. Allow yourself to feel these emotions fully, acknowledging their presence without judgment.

Identifying your passions and values is crucial. What truly ignites your soul? What matters most to you? Explore these questions thoughtfully, reflecting on past joys, forgotten dreams, and long-held aspirations. Perhaps a dormant talent is waiting to be rediscovered, or a long-forgotten dream is begging for a chance to take flight. Rediscovering these passions will not only fill your life with meaning but will also offer a sense of accomplishment and self-worth, strengthening your recovery.

Action is the bridge between intention and reality. Turn your rediscovered passions into tangible goals. Start small, setting achievable milestones that build momentum and confidence. This might involve enrolling in a class, volunteering for a cause, joining a community group, or simply committing to a daily practice that nourishes your soul, whether it's meditation, painting, or spending time in nature. The key is to consistently take steps, however small, toward a life that reflects your renewed purpose. Celebrate each victory, no matter how insignificant it may seem.

Building a supportive network is vital. Surround yourself with people who uplift and encourage you, who understand your journey and offer unconditional support. This network could include family, friends, therapists, support groups, or mentors. Share your experiences and goals, allowing others to walk alongside you, offering comfort and strength when needed. Remember, you don't have to navigate this alone; accepting help is a sign of strength, not weakness. It's crucial to foster genuine connections with people who value you and understand your needs.

Finally, remember that your renewed purpose is an ongoing evolution. It is a journey, not a destination. Your values, passions, and goals may shift and evolve as you grow and heal. Embrace this change; it's a testament to your dynamism and resilience. Celebrate the progress you've made, learn from setbacks, and trust in your ability to adapt and overcome. The path to renewed purpose is unique to you; trust in your journey, and allow your inherent strength and resilience to guide you towards a brighter future. Your story is far from over, it is merely beginning its next glorious chapter. Embrace the unfolding of your renewed purpose.

5.5 Personal Growth

Understanding personal growth isn't about magically erasing the past; it's about consciously shaping your future. It's the deliberate act of becoming a better version of yourself, a process that requires consistent effort and self-awareness. This journey, however, is not a linear path. It's filled with unexpected twists and turns, moments of profound clarity juxtaposed with periods of doubt. Embrace this inherent unpredictability; it's part of the process.

For many, personal growth begins with acknowledging the weight of the past. Previous chapters have explored the deep impact of trauma and its lasting effects. Recognizing this impact isn't about dwelling on the negativity, but about understanding its influence on your current self. This acknowledgement acts as the foundation upon which you can build a stronger, more resilient you. Consider journaling as a valuable tool to process these emotions; writing down your thoughts can provide a release and help you understand recurring patterns. This insight isn't about self-blame; rather, it's about creating a roadmap for your personal journey.

Self-compassion is not a luxury; it's a necessity. It's about treating yourself with the same kindness and understanding you'd offer a close friend struggling with similar challenges. Learn to forgive yourself for past mistakes and acknowledge your inherent worthiness of love and happiness. This doesn't mean ignoring your shortcomings; rather, it's about recognizing them without letting them define you. This journey of self-acceptance can be supported by mindfulness practices. Taking even a few minutes each day to focus on your breath, to ground yourself in the present moment, can significantly reduce anxiety and improve self-awareness. Remember, progress, not perfection, is the goal. Setting realistic goals is crucial. Don't try to overhaul your entire life overnight. Start small, setting achievable targets that gradually build your confidence and momentum. Maybe it's starting with a daily walk, reading for fifteen minutes before bed, or taking up a new hobby. These small victories, when consistently pursued, accumulate into significant personal growth. Remember that setbacks are inevitable. These aren't failures, but valuable learning experiences, opportunities to adjust your approach and try again. Each stumble provides a chance for reflection and refinement.

Building healthy relationships is paramount. Surround yourself with supportive individuals who uplift and encourage you. These connections provide a vital buffer against stress and offer valuable perspectives during challenging times. If you find yourself struggling with toxic relationships, prioritize setting healthy boundaries. Remember, it's okay to distance yourself from relationships that drain your energy and hinder your personal growth. Remember, true connection fosters growth and healing.

Finally, embrace continuous learning. Personal growth is a lifelong journey, not a destination. Remain curious, open to new experiences, and willing to challenge your beliefs. Read books, attend workshops, engage in meaningful conversations—all of these contribute to expanding your understanding of yourself and the world around you. Seek out opportunities for personal growth, both big and small. The investment in yourself will yield immeasurable rewards, providing lasting inner peace and resilience to handle whatever life throws your way. Remember, the journey towards self-discovery is unique; personalize it and celebrate your every success, large or small. This is the essence of personal growth—a journey of self-discovery and continuous evolution.

6 Chapter 6: Building Resilience

Developing resilience isn't about avoiding hardship; it's about learning to navigate it. Think of it as building a strong, flexible tree, able to bend in the wind but not break. This chapter focuses on practical strategies to fortify your emotional landscape, equipping you to face future challenges with greater composure and strength. We'll explore techniques that move beyond mere coping—we aim for genuine resilience.

Stress, in its many forms, is an unavoidable part of life. However, its impact doesn't have to be debilitating. Mastering stress management isn't about eliminating stress; it's about managing your response to it. One effective technique is mindfulness. Mindfulness isn't just about meditation; it's about cultivating a present-moment awareness. By focusing on your breath, your senses, and your immediate surroundings, you can detach from overwhelming thoughts and anxieties. Practice this regularly, even for a few minutes each day, and you'll gradually find yourself better equipped to handle stressful situations.

Regular physical activity is more than just good for your body; it's vital for mental resilience. Exercise releases endorphins, natural mood boosters that combat stress and improve your overall sense of well-being. Find activities you genuinely enjoy, whether it's a brisk walk, a dance class, or a game of tennis. The key is consistency; aim for at least 30 minutes of moderate-intensity exercise most days of the week. Remember to prioritize enjoyable activities that you'll stick with, ensuring consistent engagement.

Beyond physical exercise, incorporate practices that nourish your mind and spirit. This could involve anything from reading inspiring literature to spending time in nature, engaging in creative pursuits, or listening to calming music. These activities offer a sanctuary from stress and provide an opportunity for self-reflection and renewal. Prioritize activities that help you relax and recharge – find your personal "reset" button.

Building a strong support network is crucial. Surrounding yourself with positive, supportive individuals who understand your journey can provide invaluable emotional sustenance. Connect with friends, family, or support groups—sharing your experiences can alleviate feelings of isolation and provide encouragement during difficult times. Cultivate meaningful relationships that provide emotional stability.

Healthy boundaries are often overlooked but are essential for resilience. Learning to say no to commitments that drain your energy, protecting your time and emotional resources, allows you to prioritize your well-being. It's not selfish; it's self-preservation. Establish clear limits with healthy, balanced interaction, ensuring your personal space and well-being are respected. Learn to assert your needs effectively and respectfully.

Sleep is often underestimated in its importance to mental well-being. Aim for seven to eight hours of quality sleep each night. Establish a regular sleep schedule, create a relaxing bedtime routine, and make your bedroom a sleep-conducive environment. Adequate sleep is crucial for emotional regulation and cognitive function, improving your ability to cope with stress. A well-rested mind is a resilient mind.

Nutrition significantly impacts mental and emotional resilience. A balanced diet, rich in fruits, vegetables, and whole grains, provides the essential nutrients your body needs to function optimally. Limit processed foods, sugar, and caffeine, as these can exacerbate stress and negatively impact your mood. Focus on nourishing your body, mirroring your dedication to your emotional well-being.

Learning to forgive—yourself and others—is paramount. Holding onto resentment and anger only perpetuates suffering. Forgiveness is not about condoning harmful actions; it's about releasing the emotional burden they carry. Practice self-compassion, acknowledging your imperfections, and extending the same understanding to others.

Finally, cultivate a sense of purpose. Having meaningful goals and pursuits provides direction and motivation, particularly during challenging times. Identify your values and passions, aligning your actions with what truly matters to you. This sense of purpose anchors you, enhancing your overall resilience. This is the keystone of building a resilient self, a strong foundation for navigating future storms.

6.1 Coping Mechanisms

Developing healthy coping mechanisms is crucial for navigating life's inevitable challenges, especially after experiencing trauma. It's not about erasing the past, but about equipping yourself with tools to manage difficult emotions and situations more effectively. Think of these mechanisms as your personal toolkit, readily available whenever you need them. Learning these strategies is an ongoing process, a journey of self-discovery and empowerment. Remember that what works for one person might not work for another, so experimentation and self-awareness are key.

Identifying your triggers is the first step. What situations, thoughts, or feelings tend to overwhelm you? Keeping a journal can be incredibly helpful in this process. Note down the circumstances surrounding challenging moments, the physical sensations you experienced (like a racing heart or tense muscles), and the emotions that arose. This increased self-awareness allows you to anticipate potentially stressful situations and prepare accordingly. This detailed self-reflection is vital for personal growth and better emotional regulation. Through this process, you will gain a deeper understanding of your own responses to stressors. This knowledge is power.

Once you've identified your triggers, you can start developing specific coping mechanisms. These aren't one-size-fits-all solutions; they are personalized strategies tailored to your unique needs. For instance, if social gatherings trigger anxiety, you might practice relaxation techniques beforehand, such as deep breathing exercises or progressive muscle relaxation. If negative self-talk is a problem, challenge those thoughts actively, replacing them with more positive and realistic affirmations. Remember, it's okay to seek professional guidance in developing and refining these strategies. A therapist can provide personalized support and help you identify additional coping techniques.

Mindfulness practices, such as meditation or yoga, can be profoundly beneficial. These practices help you to focus on the present moment, reducing the power of rumination and worry about the past or future. Even a few minutes of daily meditation can make a significant difference in your ability to manage stress and regulate emotions. Start small, even five minutes a day, and gradually increase the duration as you become more comfortable. Consistency is key to reaping the full benefits of these practices. Finding a quiet space and focusing on your breath are excellent starting points. Guided meditations are readily available online or through apps.

Physical activity is another powerful coping mechanism. Exercise releases endorphins, which have mood-boosting effects. It doesn't have to be strenuous; a brisk walk, a bike ride, or even some stretching can significantly reduce stress and improve your overall mood. Find activities you enjoy and make them a regular part of your routine. The goal is to incorporate movement into your daily life, making it a positive habit that supports your mental well-being. The benefits of regular physical activity extend far beyond stress reduction; they also contribute to improved sleep, increased energy levels, and better physical health.

Social support is invaluable. Connect with friends, family, or support groups. Talking about your challenges can be incredibly cathartic, and sharing your experiences with others who understand can reduce feelings of isolation and loneliness. If you find it difficult to open up to those close to you, consider seeking professional help or joining a support group specifically designed for individuals facing similar challenges. Building strong social connections is a cornerstone of mental resilience.

Healthy lifestyle choices play a vital role in building resilience. Prioritize getting enough sleep, eating nutritious food, and limiting your intake of alcohol and caffeine. These seemingly small changes can have a significant impact on your mood, energy levels, and ability to cope with stress. Ensure your diet is balanced, incorporating plenty of fruits, vegetables, and whole grains. Aim for 7-9 hours of quality sleep each night, establishing a regular sleep schedule to regulate your circadian rhythm.

Learning to say "no" is a crucial coping skill. Setting boundaries is essential to protect your mental and emotional well-being. Don't overcommit yourself, and prioritize your own needs. Saying "no" doesn't mean being selfish; it means recognizing your limits and taking care of yourself. This is particularly important when facing overwhelming demands or situations that trigger stress or anxiety. This self-advocacy is an important part of building and maintaining your mental resilience. It empowers you to make choices that support your overall well-being.

Finally, remember that building resilience is a lifelong journey. There will be times when you feel overwhelmed, and that's perfectly okay. The important thing is to have a range of coping mechanisms at your disposal and to be kind to yourself throughout the process. Celebrate your successes, no matter how small they may seem, and remember that setbacks are opportunities for learning and growth. You are stronger than you think, and with the right tools and support, you can navigate life's challenges with greater ease and serenity.

6.2 Stress Management

Stress, a ubiquitous element of modern life, doesn't discriminate. It impacts everyone, regardless of background or circumstance. However, understanding its mechanisms and proactively implementing management techniques is crucial for maintaining mental and physical well-being, particularly after experiencing significant trauma. Learning to navigate stress effectively isn't about eliminating it entirely—a completely stress-free life is unrealistic—but rather about developing coping skills to handle inevitable challenges with resilience. This allows for a more balanced life, enabling you to process difficult emotions effectively and make more conscious choices.

Effective stress management isn't a one-size-fits-all solution. It requires a personalized approach that identifies your unique stressors and leverages strategies tailored to your individual needs and preferences. While professional guidance is always beneficial, numerous readily accessible techniques can form the foundation of your personal stress management plan. For instance, identifying your triggers is paramount. What situations, thoughts, or people consistently lead to increased feelings of tension and anxiety? This self-awareness is the first crucial step towards effective management; understanding your individual triggers is the key. Keeping a journal can provide valuable insights, detailing how you feel in various circumstances, helping to pinpoint specific stressors.

Physical activity plays a pivotal role in stress reduction. Exercise isn't just about physical health; it significantly impacts mental well-being. Engaging in regular physical activity, be it a brisk walk, a swim, or a more intense workout, releases endorphins, natural mood boosters that counter stress hormones. The type of activity doesn't have to be strenuous; finding an activity you enjoy increases the likelihood of adherence, maximizing its benefits. This simple habit, integrated into your daily routine, can make a substantial difference in your overall stress levels, significantly improving mental clarity and emotional resilience. Remember, consistency is key; even short, regular bursts of activity are more effective than infrequent, prolonged sessions.

Mindfulness practices, such as meditation or deep breathing exercises, offer another powerful approach to stress management. These techniques cultivate a state of present moment awareness, reducing rumination on past anxieties or future uncertainties. By focusing on your breath, you gently shift your attention away from stressful thoughts and feelings, creating a space for calm and clarity. Several apps and online resources offer guided meditations for beginners, making it easy to incorporate these practices into your daily routine. Even five to ten minutes of daily practice can significantly reduce stress levels and enhance overall well-being over time. Remember that consistency is more important than duration.

Prioritizing sufficient sleep is often overlooked but is crucial for stress management. Sleep deprivation amplifies stress responses, making it harder to cope with challenges. Aim for seven to nine hours of quality sleep each night. Establish a regular sleep schedule, create a relaxing bedtime routine, and optimize your sleep environment for darkness and quiet. Avoid screen time before bed, and consider incorporating relaxation techniques like warm baths or reading before sleep. Prioritizing sleep isn't a luxury; it's a necessity, especially during times of stress and trauma. The benefits to your overall emotional resilience are immense, positively influencing your capacity to navigate life's challenges. Social connection provides a vital buffer against stress. Strong social support networks provide emotional reassurance and practical assistance during challenging times. Nurturing relationships with family, friends, or support groups provides a sense of belonging and shared understanding, reducing feelings of isolation and helplessness. It is crucial to actively cultivate these relationships; investing time in meaningful connections is an investment in your mental health. Regular communication, shared activities, and open dialogue are vital elements in building resilient social support networks. These connections serve as anchors during periods of stress, offering emotional sustenance and practical support.

Finally, remember that seeking professional help is a sign of strength, not weakness. Therapists provide a safe and supportive space to explore your stress responses, develop effective coping strategies, and process past traumas that might contribute to your stress levels. Therapy offers personalized guidance and support, tailored to your individual needs and experiences. Don't hesitate to reach out for help if you feel overwhelmed; it's a proactive step towards improved mental and emotional well-being. There's no shame in seeking professional support; it's a vital part of a comprehensive approach to effective stress management.

7 Chapter 7: Living with Serenity

Cultivating serenity isn't about ignoring life's complexities; it's about learning to navigate them with grace and composure. It's about finding a quiet strength within yourself, a wellspring of peace that can weather any storm. This doesn't mean you'll never feel sadness or anger—those are natural human emotions. Serenity is the ability to acknowledge those emotions without letting them consume you, to find a center of calm amidst the chaos. It is the gentle acceptance of what is, while simultaneously working towards what can be.

Practicing gratitude is a cornerstone of this peaceful existence. It's easy to focus on what's missing, on the hardships endured, but shifting your perspective to appreciate the small joys, the simple blessings—a warm cup of tea, a sunny day, a kind word from a friend—can significantly alter your emotional landscape.

Gratitude isn't about ignoring the difficulties; it's about acknowledging them while simultaneously appreciating the good things you have. Keep a gratitude journal, jotting down even the smallest things you are grateful for. This simple act can gradually shift your mindset towards positivity and contentment, fostering a sense of inner peace. Over time, this practice will become a powerful tool for resilience and emotional well-being.
The future, after surviving trauma, often feels uncertain, even daunting. Fear of relapse or the shadow of past pain can loom large. However, approaching the future with hope, not fear, is crucial for lasting serenity. This doesn't mean ignoring potential challenges; it's about facing them with a newfound strength, knowing you've already overcome so much. Visualize your ideal future—what does it look like? What does it feel like? By actively creating a vision of serenity and happiness, you lay the groundwork for its manifestation. This forward-looking approach helps reframe your narrative from one of survival to one of thriving. It empowers you to take proactive steps towards building the life you desire, shifting your focus from the past to the potential of the future. This sense of purpose and anticipation fuels your journey towards a peaceful and fulfilling life.
Remember, serenity is not a destination but a journey, an ongoing process of self-discovery and self-acceptance. It's a state

of being you cultivate through consistent practice and self-compassion. There will be moments when your peace is challenged, when old wounds resurface. That's okay. Acknowledge those moments, allow yourself to feel them, and then gently guide yourself back to your center of calm. Use the coping mechanisms you've developed, the mindfulness techniques you've learned, and the support systems you've built. These resources are your allies in this ongoing journey. Maintaining your serenity is a testament to your strength, your resilience, and your unwavering commitment to a peaceful and fulfilling life. The path to serenity is paved with self-awareness, mindful practices, and a persistent commitment to your well-being. It's a journey that requires both courage and compassion.

This isn't a race; it's about finding a sustainable rhythm of self-care and emotional regulation. Small, consistent actions—a daily meditation, a brief walk in nature, spending time with loved ones, engaging in hobbies you enjoy—make a profound difference over time. Prioritize self-care as if your life depends on it, because in a way, it does. Treat yourself with the same kindness and understanding you would offer a close friend. Engage in activities that nourish your soul, that bring you joy and a sense of purpose. These actions are not indulgences; they're essential components of a life lived with serenity, a life free from the relentless grip of past traumas. Your well-being is paramount, a precious gift you must nurture. Living with serenity isn't about escaping life's challenges; it's about facing them with quiet strength, a steady hand on the rudder of your own life.

Living serenely doesn't mean erasing the past; it means integrating it into your narrative, learning from it, and allowing it to shape you into a stronger, wiser, more compassionate individual. It's about finding peace amidst the storm, a quiet strength within the chaos. It's a journey that unfolds one moment at a time, one breath at a time, one act of self-compassion at a time. Embrace this journey with open arms and an unwavering commitment to your well-being. Your path to serenity is unique, personal, and ultimately, empowering. The serenity you cultivate is a beacon of hope, not just for yourself, but for others who may be walking a similar path. Your resilience is an inspiration, a testament to the human spirit's capacity for healing and growth. The ultimate gift is this newfound peace, a tranquility borne from the crucible of past experiences, a quiet strength that allows you to live each day with gratitude, hope, and a deep sense of inner calm.

7.1 Peaceful Existence

Cultivating inner peace isn't about ignoring life's complexities; it's about learning to navigate them with grace and resilience. Imagine a calm lake, reflecting the sky, even as the wind ruffles its surface. That's the essence of peaceful existence – finding stillness amidst the chaos. This doesn't mean eliminating all stress or hardship; those are inevitable aspects of the human experience. Instead, it's about fostering a mental state where you can weather the storms without being capsized.

Consider practicing mindfulness, a technique previously introduced, but now focused on its application in daily life. Start small – noticing the sensation of your breath, the taste of your food, or the warmth of the sun on your skin. These simple acts ground you in the present, preventing your mind from wandering into anxieties about the future or regrets about the past. This consistent engagement with the present moment acts as an anchor, steadying you during turbulent times. The key is regular practice; even five minutes a day can make a significant difference in your overall sense of calm. This isn't just a fleeting feeling; consistent practice transforms your relationship with your inner self and the world around you. The more you engage with the present, the less power the past and future hold over your emotional well-being.

Forgiveness, another crucial element explored earlier, takes on a new dimension when seeking peace. Forgiveness isn't condoning harmful actions; it's releasing yourself from the burden of resentment and anger. Holding onto negativity consumes your energy and prevents you from moving forward. Forgiving others, and importantly, forgiving yourself, frees you to experience the lightness of peace. Start by acknowledging the hurt you've experienced; validating those feelings is the first step towards letting them go. Then, consciously choose to release the anger or resentment. This is not a passive process; it requires conscious effort and, perhaps, professional guidance. But the rewards are immeasurable – a freeing up of emotional energy that can be redirected towards nurturing your inner serenity. Remember, forgiveness is a gift you give yourself, allowing you to move forward and embrace a more peaceful future.

Gratitude, often underestimated, is a powerful tool for cultivating peace. Regularly taking time to appreciate the good things in your life, no matter how small, shifts your focus from what you lack to what you have. This simple act reframes your perspective, fostering a more positive outlook. Begin a gratitude journal, noting down three things you're thankful for each day. It could be anything, from a sunny day to a supportive friend, a warm cup of coffee, or simply the ability to breathe. The act of recording your gratitude solidifies it in your mind, reinforcing the positive feelings. Gradually, this practice will become a habit, shaping your thoughts and emotions in a way that fosters inner peace. Over time, you'll find that your perspective changes; the challenges remain, but their impact is lessened by a constant awareness of the good in your life.

Finding a supportive community is essential. Sharing your experiences with others who understand can provide validation, reduce feelings of isolation, and offer practical advice. This could involve joining a support group, connecting with friends or family, or seeking guidance from a spiritual leader. Remember, you don't have to navigate your journey alone. The support of others creates a sense of belonging, reducing feelings of loneliness and enhancing your sense of security. Engage in activities that bring you joy and connect you with others who share your interests. Whether it's joining a book club, volunteering, or participating in a sports team, these connections offer opportunities for shared experiences, mutual support, and a sense of community.

Building a life of peaceful existence isn't a destination; it's an ongoing journey. It requires consistent effort, self-awareness, and a commitment to nurturing your inner well-being. Embrace the challenges as opportunities for growth, celebrate your successes, and remember that even amidst the storms, you can find your own personal oasis of calm. The pursuit of peace is a lifelong endeavor, but the rewards—a sense of inner serenity, resilience in the face of adversity, and the ability to live a fulfilling life—make the journey worthwhile. Remember the techniques discussed throughout this book; they are tools for your personal growth, tools to help you build a more peaceful and meaningful life.

7.2 Gratitude's Embrace

Focusing on what we have, rather than what we lack, shifts our perspective dramatically. This isn't about ignoring hardship; it's about acknowledging it alongside the good. Think of it like this: even on the darkest night, there are still stars. Finding and appreciating those stars, those small moments of joy, is the essence of cultivating gratitude. It's a conscious choice, a daily practice that strengthens our resilience and deepens our sense of peace. It's not a magical cure-all, but a powerful tool in our healing journey. It's about actively seeking out the positive, no matter how small it may seem.

The benefits of gratitude extend far beyond simply feeling happier. Studies show a strong correlation between gratitude and improved physical health. Individuals who regularly practice gratitude often report better sleep, reduced blood pressure, and an enhanced immune system. This isn't just anecdotal; research backs up these claims, demonstrating a measurable physiological impact. The very act of appreciating the good in our lives triggers positive chemical reactions in our brains, creating a cascade of well-being. And that well-being, that sense of contentment, is a vital part of our recovery.

Start small. Begin by keeping a gratitude journal. Each day, jot down three things you're thankful for. These could be anything—a warm cup of tea on a cold morning, a supportive friend, the beauty of a sunset. Don't overthink it; just write what comes naturally. The act of writing itself helps to solidify the feeling of gratitude, making it more ingrained in your daily experience. This simple practice, repeated daily, can bring about surprisingly profound changes over time. It allows us to actively shift our focus from the negative to the positive.

Gratitude isn't about ignoring pain or pretending it doesn't exist. It's about acknowledging the pain alongside the good, recognizing that even in difficult times, there are things to be thankful for. This is particularly crucial after experiencing trauma. The tendency is to focus on the negative, to dwell on what was lost. However, by actively practicing gratitude, you counter this tendency. You develop a more balanced perspective, capable of recognizing both light and shadow. This balance allows for healing to take place in a healthy manner.

Sometimes, it feels impossible to find something to be grateful for. During these times, it's essential to practice self-compassion. Don't beat yourself up for struggling; recognize that gratitude is a skill that requires practice. Start by focusing on basic things – the simple things: your own breath, a functioning body, a roof over your head. These may seem trivial, but they are essential, and appreciating them is a powerful first step. Gradually, as you gain momentum, you will find it easier to notice and appreciate more significant aspects of your life.

Gratitude is a journey, not a destination. There will be days when it feels easy, and days when it feels challenging. The key is to remain consistent, to make it a regular part of your routine. Like any muscle, gratitude strengthens with use. The more you practice it, the easier it becomes to find the good, even amid adversity. It becomes an intrinsic part of your being, a lens through which you view the world—a world that often feels broken, but is still filled with beauty, and kindness, and possibility. This will improve your overall outlook and help you to find that inner serenity that so many struggle to find.

Beyond personal journaling, expressing gratitude to others can be equally transformative. A simple "thank you" can have a profound impact, both on the recipient and on the giver. It strengthens relationships, fosters connections, and promotes a sense of community. This act of outward gratitude can have ripple effects, leading to a broader sense of well-being and interconnectedness—a sense of belonging that is invaluable in the healing process. It's also a great way to build stronger relationships with people who care about you.

Incorporating gratitude into your daily life might involve simple acts such as sending thank-you notes, expressing appreciation to loved ones, or simply taking a moment to appreciate the natural world. These small gestures of appreciation create a ripple effect, positively impacting not only your own well-being but also the lives of others. The practice of gratitude isn't just a personal endeavor; it's a social one, strengthening the bonds that support our healing and overall mental health. This approach leads to a more positive cycle.

Remember, the path to serenity is not always linear. There will be setbacks, moments of doubt, and times when the weight of the past feels overwhelming. But by embracing gratitude, you cultivate a resilience that can carry you through these challenges. It's a lifeline, a source of strength that helps you to navigate the difficult terrain and to find moments of joy, even in the midst of suffering. It is an anchor in the storm.

Ultimately, gratitude's embrace isn't just about feeling good; it's about fostering a deep and meaningful connection with life, with yourself, and with others. It's about recognizing the inherent goodness in the world, even when it's hard to see. It's about finding the light within yourself and letting it shine. It allows us to heal emotionally. It brings peace. And ultimately, it guides us towards a more serene and fulfilling existence. Through consistent practice, it will change your life.

7.3 Future's Promise

The journey, arduous as it's been, doesn't conclude with the achievement of serenity. It's a continuous unfolding, a constant refinement of the self, a persistent nurturing of the inner peace you've painstakingly cultivated. Think of it like a garden – you've cleared the weeds, tilled the soil, planted the seeds of hope, and now you must tend to it, ensuring it flourishes. This requires ongoing commitment, consistent effort, and a willingness to adapt as life inevitably throws new challenges your way. Remember the strength you've discovered within, the resilience you've built.

This isn't about arriving at a static destination; it's about embracing the ongoing process of growth. The future isn't a blank canvas, a pristine white space awaiting your masterpiece. Instead, it's a vibrant, evolving landscape, filled with opportunities and, yes, inevitable uncertainties. The key lies in approaching those uncertainties not with fear, but with the wisdom and self-awareness you've gained. Your past experiences, though painful, have shaped you, forged you into someone stronger, more compassionate, and more resilient.

Embrace the unknown with a sense of curious anticipation, rather than trepidation. Consider setting small, achievable goals. These might be related to personal projects you've put aside, relationships you've longed to mend, or skills you've always wanted to learn. The accomplishment of these small victories will further boost your self-esteem and reinforce your belief in your own capabilities, building momentum toward larger aspirations. Don't overwhelm yourself; steady, consistent progress is far more sustainable and ultimately more rewarding than sporadic bursts of intense activity.

Remember the importance of self-care. This is not a luxury, but a necessity, the very foundation upon which your continued well-being rests. Maintain healthy habits—nourishing your body with healthy food, engaging in regular physical activity, and prioritizing adequate sleep. These practices aren't just about physical health; they significantly impact your mental and emotional well-being too. A healthy mind and body are better equipped to navigate life's inevitable challenges with grace and resilience. Cultivate meaningful relationships. Surround yourself with people who uplift you, who support your growth, and who offer unconditional love and acceptance. These connections are essential for your continued healing and provide a vital buffer against future stressors. Nurture these bonds, communicate openly and honestly, and don't hesitate to seek support when you need it. Remember that vulnerability is a sign of strength, not weakness. Continue practicing mindfulness and self-compassion. These are not quick fixes; they are lifelong practices requiring consistent effort. The more you integrate these techniques into your daily life, the better equipped you will be to manage stress, regulate emotions, and navigate life's inevitable challenges. Regular meditation, mindful breathing, and self-reflective journaling can all contribute significantly to this ongoing process.

The future holds immense potential, a promise of joy, fulfillment, and continued growth. This promise isn't a guarantee; it's an invitation, a challenge to actively participate in shaping your own destiny. By drawing on the strength you've discovered, the resilience you've cultivated, and the serenity you've attained, you can navigate whatever life throws your way, emerging stronger, wiser, and more fulfilled than ever before. This is not just a chapter's end, but a new beginning, a testament to your enduring spirit. Remember the pain you've overcome; let it fuel your journey towards a brighter, more hopeful future. The path ahead may be unknown, but you are now equipped to walk it with confidence, grace, and unwavering self-belief. The future is yours to shape; embrace its promise.

www.ingramcontent.com/pod-product-compliance
Lightning Source LLC
LaVergne TN
LVHW022007200926
848481LV00007B/2269
9798349451898